PIONEER VALLEY

SNOWBOARDING

SEAN FINNIGAN

TABLE OF CONTENTS

The History of Snowboarding 4
The Feud on Snow 8
Jibbing 12
Freestyle 14
Snowboarding Gear 16
Snowboard Safety 18
Glossary/Index 20

How would you like to fly down a snow-covered mountain balancing on a board attached to your feet? If you think that would be fun, then snowboarding might be the sport for you!

3

THE HISTORY OF SNOWBOARDING

The first snowboard was called a "Snurfer." The Snurfer was a skateboard without wheels. You steered the Snurfer down a snow-covered hill with a rope. Everyone who tried the Snurfer loved it.

Soon there were Snurfing **competitions**. People came from all over the country to take part in the competitions.

Soon, other people began to design and make snowboards as well.

Snowboarding became more and more popular.

New and better snowboards were made for the sport.

The first world championship snowboarding event was held in 1938. In 1998, snowboarding became a Winter Olympic sport.

THE FEUD ON SNOW

At first, skiers did not like snowboarders. Many ski resorts did not allow snowboarding. Skiers believed the snowboarders scraped off the best snow and were a danger to others on the mountain.

Snowboarders found other places to snowboard. More and more young people started snowboarding. Some ski resorts thought snowboarding was just a passing **fad.** They did not want to lose their regular ski customers, so they **banned** snowboarders from their resorts.

Then it became clear that snowboarding was here to stay. Some ski resorts built special areas where snowboarders could perform their jumps without getting in the way of skiers. More and more people went to these ski resorts.

Now, most ski slopes allow snowboarding.

11

JIBBING

A jib is something a snowboarder does tricks on, such as a rail or a log. When a snowboarder jumps, slides, or rides on top of a jib, it is called jibbing.

13

FREESTYLE

Freestyle snowboarding is done with man-made objects, such as rails, jumps, and boxes. The freestyle snowboarder slides across the objects to do tricks. Freestyle snowboarders also use a **halfpipe**. A halfpipe is a trench-like half tube made of snow.

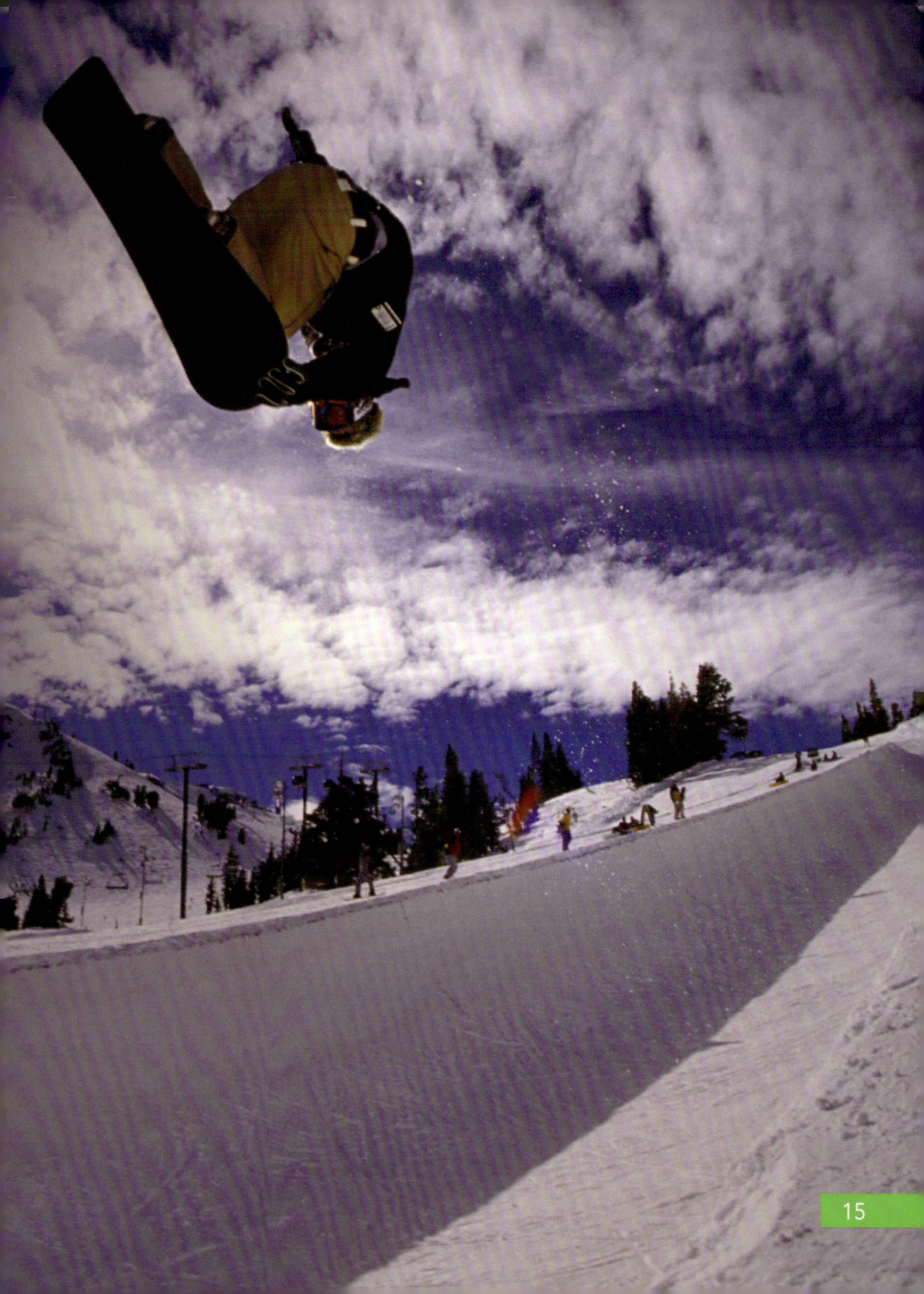

SNOWBOARDING GEAR

There are several different kinds of snowboards. Each has a special shape that allows the snowboarder to do different kinds of riding.

A snowboarder wears special boots that slip into bindings on the board. Helmets and goggles are also important for helping keep a snowboarder safe.

goggles — helmet

binding

boot

snowboard

17

SNOWBOARD SAFETY

People can get injured snowboarding.

It is important to be careful when snowboarding to keep yourself from getting hurt. Most snowboarders who do get hurt are beginners.

It is important to take lessons from an instructor.

It is also important to wear a helmet.

A helmet protects a snowboarder's head if he or she falls.

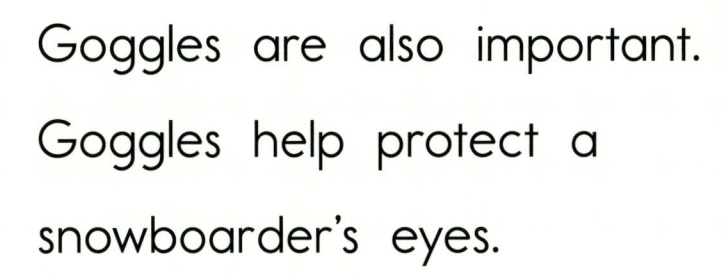

Goggles are also important. Goggles help protect a snowboarder's eyes.

GLOSSARY

banned: prohibited, forbidden, or barred

competitions: contests where someone is trying to win something that someone else is also trying to win

fad: a practice or interest followed for a time with exaggerated zeal

freestyle: a competition in which the competitors are allowed to use different styles or methods

halfpipe: a trench-like half tube made of snow

INDEX

banned 9
competitions 5
fad 9
freestyle 14
goggles 16-17, 19
halfpipe 14
instructor 8

jib 12
mountain 2, 8
slopes 10
snowboards 5, 6, 16
Snurfer 4
sport 2, 6-7
Winter Olympic 7